FROM

TO

Prayers

FROM A
CHILD'S HEART

A delightful read-along book
that will help young children learn to pray.

Joni
EARECKSON
TADA

FrontPorch
BOOKS

PRAYERS FROM A CHILD'S HEART
by Joni Eareckson Tada

Copyright ©1999 FrontPorch Books,
a division of Garborg's LLC

Design by Koechel Peterson & Associates
Photography by Tom Henry, Koechel Peterson & Associates

Published by Garborg's LLC
P. O. Box 20132
Bloomington, MN 55420

Scripture quotations are taken from The Holy Bible,
New International Version®. Copyright ©1973,
1978, 1984 by International Bible Society.
Used by permission of Zondervan Publishing House.

ISBN 1-58375-474-1

Contents

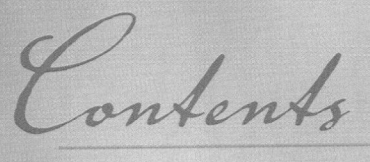

Introduction	7
Spring Time	9
Heaven	10-11
Obedience	13
Precious in His Sight	14
Fall	16
God's Protection	18-19
Obedience	20
Family	22
Fear	24
Awesome God	25
Come Into My Heart	27
Loving God	28
Parents	31
God Loves Us	33
Thankfulness	34-35
Friends	36
Be Kind	39
Kindness	39
Creation	40
Forgiveness	41
Snow	42
Hearing God	44
Filled With God	45
Family	47
Joy	49
Helping Others	49
God's Help	50-51
God Cares for Me	52
Contentment	54-55
Prayer for Poor People	56
Peace	56
Bible	58-59
Jesus Died for Me	61
Following God	61
Missionaries	62
Praying for Others	63
Church	64

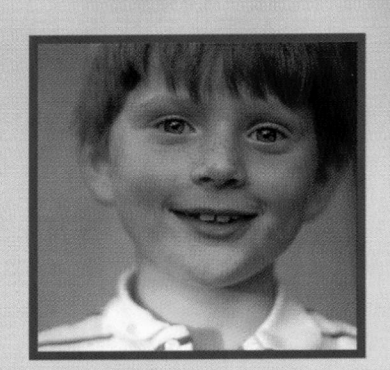

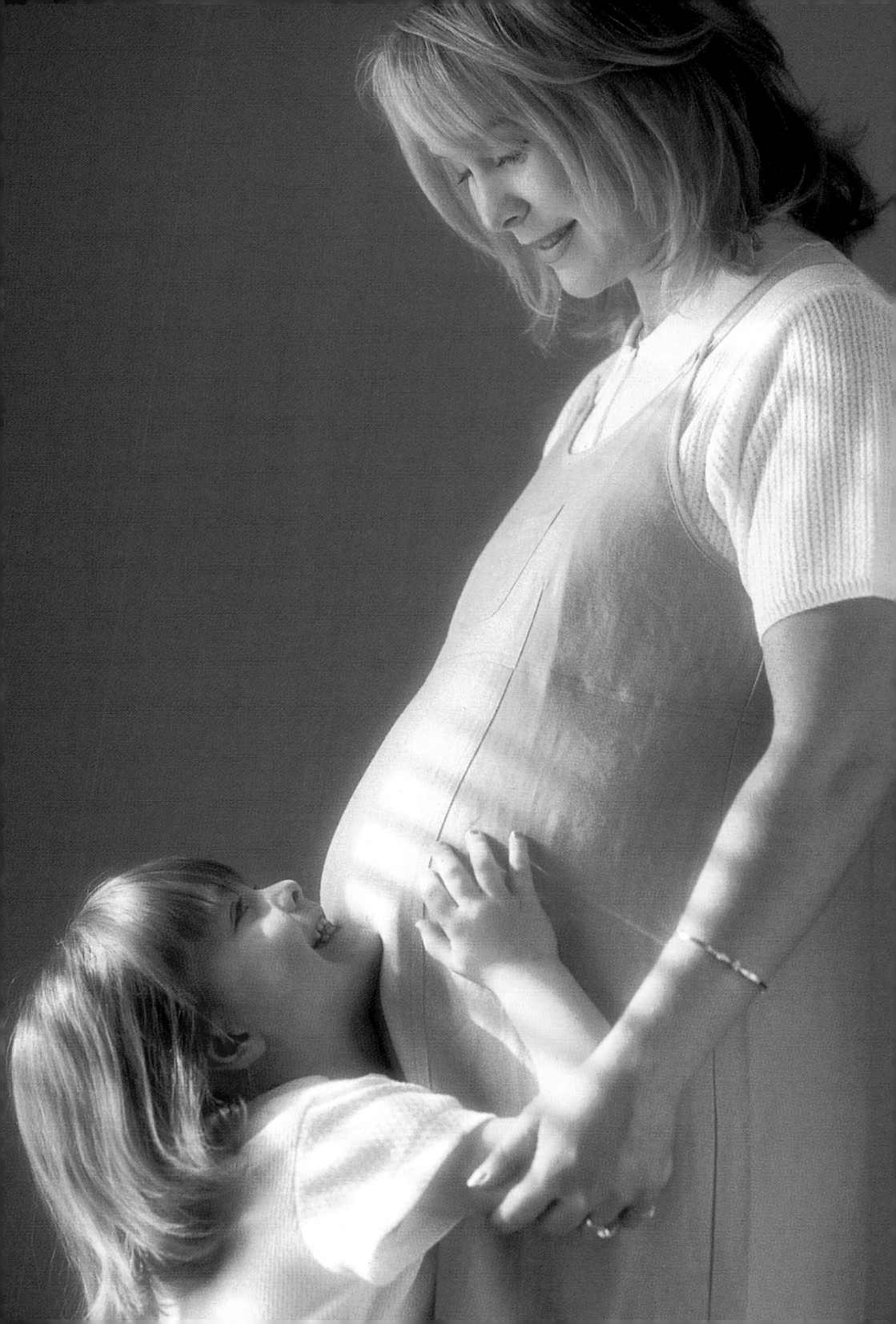

Introduction

WHAT COULD BE MORE IRRESISTIBLE THAN A CHILD'S PURE, honest prayer? God treasures these simple, heartfelt prayers and calls parents to lead their little ones toward Him. "Let the little children come to me," Jesus says, "and do not stop them, for the kingdom of God belongs to such as these." (Mark 10:14)

Help your children learn how to express in words the prayers of their heart by praying with them regularly. Take a few moments together each day, perhaps before breakfast or bed, to read a verse and prayer from these pages. Let the words inspire your own prayers and encourage your little ones to pray. Simple moments like these will not only teach your children the importance of talking with God, but will touch your heart and His.

Spring Time

He will come to us

  like the winter rains,

    like the spring rains

      that water the earth.

HOSEA 6:3

SPRING IS IN FULL BLOOM…AND IT'S GREAT! THE EARTH looks like it's going to burst with all the brand new flowers and the trees with their little green leaves. God, I think You must have smiled a lot when You made the flowers. It's amazing when You look real close at a rose petal. It feels so soft and it has little tiny veins and it smells like perfume.

You drench its furrows and level its ridges;

  you soften it with showers and bless its crops.

PSALM 65:10

THE FARMERS ARE PLANTING LOTS OF SEEDS RIGHT NOW, and they are hoping that lots of things grow. I pray for the sun to shine and the rain to fall on the new little seeds so that all of us will have food to eat. It's great to enjoy the world You created.

Heaven

For here we do not have an enduring city,

but we are looking for the city that is to come.

HEBREWS 13:14

LORD, HEAVEN IS BEING WHERE YOU ARE FOREVER. WHEN I LOOK up at the stars at night, it almost looks like the sky is on fire. It's fantastic to think that one day I'll be up there with You. You will welcome us home, and, boy, what a party that is going to be! Thank You for being such a wonderful father.

For the Lord himself will come down from heaven....

We who are still alive and are left will be

caught up together with them in the clouds

to meet the Lord in the air.

And so we will be with the Lord forever.

1 THESSALONIANS 4:16-17

LORD, THE BIBLE SAYS THAT ONE DAY IN THE FUTURE THERE'S going to be a big celebration in heaven. Jesus, I'm so glad I'll finally get to see You, my best friend. I'll have a brand new body and I'll be able to jump and run like I do now—only better and faster. Thank You, Lord, for taking all of eternity to think up exciting stuff for us to do.

Do not let your hearts be troubled.

Trust in God; trust also in me.

In my Father's house are many rooms;

if it were not so, I would have told you.

I am going there to prepare a place for you....

I will come back and take you to be with me.

JOHN 14:1-3

GOD, YOU MADE THE EARTH IN JUST SEVEN DAYS. NOW I'M thinking about how long it's taking You to make a place in heaven for me. If earth is this neat, I can't imagine what heaven is like! Thank You for choosing me to be a part of Your big wide wonderful heaven.

Obedience

*Children, obey your parents
in everything, for this
pleases the Lord.*

Colossians 3:20

WAS IT HARD FOR YOU TO OBEY YOUR MOM WHEN YOU were a little boy, Jesus? Just like You, I want to do what's right. Help me to do the things I have to do around my house with a smile. Help me to be sweet like a bee, happy like a dog, and quick like a horse to do what You want.

*You are my portion, O Lord;
I have promised to obey your words.*

Psalm 119:57

I LIKE THE STORY OF THE BATTLE OF JERICHO WHERE the walls came a-tumbling down. Walking around the city so many times probably seemed silly to the people. But they obeyed and look what happened! I want to do whatever You want. I want to have a good attitude and obey with a smile, Jesus.

Precious in His Sight

How priceless is your unfailing love!

Both high and low among men

find refuge in the shadow of your wings.

PSALM 36:7

THERE'S A COUNTRY WE CALL INDIA WHERE ELEPHANTS and tigers and Brahman bulls live. Millions of people are crowded together in India, and many of them are children who live in the streets and beg. I pray for the children of India tonight.

God our Savior...wants all men to be saved

and to come to a knowledge of the truth.

For there is one God and one mediator

between God and men, the man Christ Jesus.

1 TIMOTHY 2:3-5

JAPAN IS A LITTLE COUNTRY. MANY OF THE PEOPLE WHO LIVE there spend a lot of time working. God, please help people in Japan to take time to get to know and love You. I pray that people around the world will stop believing in false gods. I pray that You will help them to know Jesus in a special and personal way.

fall

He has shown kindness by

giving you rain from heaven

and crops in their seasons;

he provides you with

plenty of food and

fills your hearts with joy.

ACTS 14:17

THE FARMERS ARE GATHERING THEIR HARVEST right now, Lord. I know it takes a lot of hard work to bring in all the grain and vegetables. I pray that they will have a good harvest. They have to work really hard, and sometimes the weather gets so bad that nothing will grow. Help them to trust you for just the right amount of rain and sun. Please put your arms around them and hold them close to You.

God's Protection

He will not let your foot slip—

  he who watches over you will not slumber.

IT'S WONDERFUL TO THINK ABOUT HOW YOU KEPT DANIEL safe in the Lion's den. Thanks for keeping me safe from danger like when You take care of me when I'm asleep. The Bible says that You never sleep and that You are always awake. You take care of everything, even the little animals in the forest. You're the one who keeps me safe.

God is our refuge and strength,

  an ever-present help in trouble.

PSALM 46:1

I LIKE WATCHING MY SHADOW WHEN IT'S A SUNNY DAY. The Bible says that we can run for cover in your shadow and You will protect us. I'm glad Your shadow is always there, no matter whether it's sunny or rainy. Thank You for protecting me from scary stuff like snakes, spiders, and lightning. Those things remind me that You're the one who keeps me safe. Thank You for taking care of me.

Keep me as the apple of your eye;

       hide me in the shadow of your wings.

PSALM 17:8

JESUS, SOMEDAY SOON I'LL START SCHOOL. I FEEL EXCITED AND scared all at once. Would You please help me to like it and to make new friends? Lord, I pray for the crossing guards at school, too. They help a lot of kids cross streets and they protect them from traffic. I pray for their safety tonight.

Obedience

Listen, my son, to your father's instruction
and do not forsake your mother's teaching.

PROVERBS 1:8

JESUS, WHAT KIND OF CHORES DID YOU DO
when You were my age? I want to do my chores with
a smile because they teach me how to be helpful and
responsible. Help me to say "Yes!" with a smile when
my mom tells me what to do.

Family

Live in harmony with one another; be sympathetic,

love as brothers, be compassionate and humble.

1 PETER 3:8

LORD, OF ALL THE PEOPLE IN THE WORLD, YOU CHOSE BROTHERS and sisters for me to be closest to. It's neat being a brother or a sister to another kid. Cousins are great too, Lord! They're a lot of fun—I wish I could see them more often. I want to tell You how much I love my aunts and uncles; thank You for giving them to me. God bless all my family.

And, Jesus, I'm so glad that You are like a big older brother who is the wisest, bravest, kindest, best brother a kid could have.

A friend loves at all times,

and a brother is born for adversity.

PROVERBS 17:17

GOD, HAVING YOU FOR MY FATHER IS THE BEST THING THAT could have ever happened in my life. Thank You for letting me be in Your family. Thank You for my family, too. Lord, I know You want families to love each other. Help families to stick together through hard times so that they will be strong in Your love. Help families everywhere, Lord.

Fear

You are my hiding place;

you will protect me from trouble

and surround me with songs of deliverance.

PSALM 32:7

I'M SOMETIMES AFRAID. BUT IT SAYS IN THE BIBLE THAT You are my hiding place. That means I can run to You whenever I feel scared. Help me not to be scared of things that You're in control of. Would You please chase those fears away? Thank You for being a safe place for me to hide.

The Lord is my light and my salvation—

whom shall I fear?

The Lord is the stronghold of my life—

of whom shall I be afraid?

PSALM 27:1

DEAR LORD, I DON'T LIKE NIGHTMARES. THEY MAKE ME UPSET. Some kids believe that monsters live under their beds. I know that's not true, but sometimes I'm still scared of the dark. Help me to remember that You're right here next to me making everything light and bright. Thanks for watching over my family and me.

Awesome God

You discern my going out and my lying down;

  you are familiar with all my ways....

    You hem me in—behind and before.

Psalm 139:3,5

Lord, I hear people say that You are the Alpha and Omega, the First and the Last, the Beginning and the End. You are every-where all at the same time. Besides that, You know everything. God, You are...awesome!

Come Into My Heart

For it is with your heart that you believe and are justified.

ROMANS 10:10

GOD, THERE ARE LITTLE KIDS LIKE ME ALL OVER the world who are asking You to come into their hearts. I want You in my heart, too. I want it to be Your home.

Loving God

Love the Lord your God with all your heart

and with all your soul and with

all your strength and with all your mind.

LUKE 10:27

JESUS, I LOVE YOU. AND I LOVE TO LISTEN TO YOU. YOU ARE GREAT and full of kindness. You are strong and powerful and gentle. The Bible says that I am supposed to love You with all my heart and soul and mind and strength. Help me to love You with everything I've got because You are the best, Jesus. I love You!

How great is the love the Father has lavished on us,

that we should be called children of God!

And that is what we are!

1 JOHN 3:1

WHEN MY MOM HUGS ME OR MY TEACHER SMILES AT ME, it makes me feel warm and special. God, I can't hug You, but here's my heart. They say that You live in my heart. But sometimes the space in my heart feels very small and You are so big. Just in case no one else in the whole wide world has said this to You today, Lord, I want to say it to You right now: I love You!

Parents

My Presence will go with you,
and I will give you rest.

EXODUS 33:14

LORD, I DON'T LIKE IT WHEN I GET SICK—ESPECIALLY when my stomach is upset. But thank You for giving me someone as special as my mom to help me feel better. Once in a while I see Mom and Dad feeling sad. Help me cheer them up when they're feeling sad. Help me to be a comfort to them like they are to me.

Honor your father and your mother,
so that you may live long in the land
the Lord your God is giving you.

EXODUS 20:12

THE TEN COMMANDMENTS ARE YOUR RULES FOR US so that we can love You, help others, and be happy. One of the commandments says, "Honor your father and mother." I don't understand why my parents say "no" sometimes. Teach me to trust them and believe that what they say is best for me.

God Loves Us

We know and rely on the love God has for us.
God is love. Whoever lives in love lives in God,
and God in him.

1 JOHN 4:16

SOMETIMES WHEN IT'S COLD, I NEED EXTRA BLANKETS ON MY BED, Lord. And sometimes when I'm feeling cold and lonely, I need extra love. Thank You that Your love is the biggest, best blanket ever! Thank You for loving and watching over us.

Jesus loves the little children, all the children of the world. Red and yellow, black and white, they are precious in His sight. Jesus loves the little children of the world.

Jesus said, "Let the little children come to me,
and do not hinder them for the kingdom of heaven
belongs to such as these."

MATTHEW 19:14

I'M GLAD YOU MADE PUPPIES AND KITTENS, BABY HORSES and bunnies, Lord. They remind me that You really love small things. Like me! God, You're so big and my voice is so small. I don't understand how You hear me, but I'm sure glad You do.

Thankfulness

The God who made the world and everything in it
is the Lord of heaven and earth....
He...gives all men life and breath and everything else.

ACTS 17:24-25

LORD, THE PRAYER YOU GAVE TO THE DISCIPLES SAYS, "Give us this day our daily bread." Thank You for giving us all the good things on our plates tonight at dinner. Thank You for soft, chocolate chip cookies fresh out of the oven and for mozzarella cheese that oozes off my pizza. Thank You for time to go to bed and sleep. Thank You for the sunshine that keeps us warm. Thank You for giving me time to play. . . and friends to play with!

Always giving thanks to God the Father for everything,
in the name of our Lord Jesus Christ.

EPHESIANS 5:20

THANK YOU FOR TIME TO GO TO BED AND SLEEP. WHEN I SLEEP, my body has a chance to rest. I think it's fantastic that You made the nighttime so that we could go to sleep. Thank You for books, Lord. We wouldn't be able to learn about things as well without them. There are so many great books to look at and read. And most of all, Lord, thank You for dying on the cross for my sins. Because of that, I can now spend eternity with You!

Today in the town of David a Savior has been born to you;
he is Christ the Lord. This will be a sign to you:
You will find a baby wrapped in cloths
and lying in a manger.

LUKE 2:11-12

JESUS, THE BIBLE TELLS US ABOUT A LOT OF MIRACLES THAT You did. Thank You that You work miracles in my life, too. I think the greatest miracle of all is that You, our great big God who created the universe, became a baby. I'm so glad You came. I'm so glad You loved us enough to send Your Son to us on earth in the form of a baby. Thank You God.

friends

*There is a friend who
sticks closer than a brother.*

PROVERBS 18:24

GOD, I'M THANKFUL THAT YOU FILLED MY WORLD WITH LOTS
and lots of friends, each and every one of them. I just want
You to know that I think one of Your very best ideas is friends.
I love it when my best friend and I get to spend a whole day
together. That must be how You feel when Your friends come
and spend time with You. I want to be your friend!

*Dear friends, let us love one another, for love
comes from God. Everyone who loves has been
born of God and knows God.*

1 JOHN 4:7

GOD, FRIENDS ARE NEAT. THEY'LL PICK YOU FIRST WHEN
choosing sides in a game, they'll invite you over when their
dog has pups, and they'll be proud of you when you do a
good job. I love my friends. Thank You for them. If I tell
You the names of my best friends, will You bless them in a
special way? Well, here they are...

Be Kind

Therefore, as we have opportunity,
let us do good to all people.

GALATIANS 6:10

HELP ME TO REMEMBER THAT THERE ARE LOTS OF PEOPLE who are feeling lonely or hurting. There are soldiers across the ocean who are feeling lonely and a kid in our neighborhood that no one seems to like. I want to be loving to those around me and pray for those across the ocean.

Kindness

Love your neighbor as yourself.

JAMES 2:8

LORD, PLEASE BE WITH THE PEOPLE WHO LIVE NEXT DOOR. I pray that they'll be safe and that they'll enjoy having us as their neighbors. Maybe we can make cookies for them this week! There's also an older person who lives nearby, and sometimes I think that person must feel lonely. I want to make sure that I pray for that person often and visit him when I can.

Creation

God made the wild animals...and all the creatures
that move along the ground....
And God saw that it was good.

Genesis 1:25

I'M IMPRESSED, GOD! I'VE BEEN THINKING ABOUT YOUR sunsets and the hundreds of animals and birds and flowers You made. You had a wonderful idea when You created camels. They are so funny looking, Lord! Bugs like fireflies and caterpillars and grasshoppers are fun to watch, too. And what about ladybugs and praying mantises? Are ladybugs really ladies and do praying mantises really pray? Your creation amazes me!

Do you know how God controls the clouds
and makes his lightning flash?

Job 37:15

I LOVE A HOT SUMMER DAY, LORD. AND I LOVE WALKING BAREFOOT so I can feel the grass and dirt on my feet. I love splashing in a stream and taking a nap under a big tree. And when it's really hot out, Lord, I'm especially glad that You invented water. Swimming is fun. It feels so good! I like the cold seasons, too, Lord. For when the weather turns cool, it reminds me that You are in charge of the seasons. I'm excited about the change in seasons. Thank You for the way You always make our world so interesting.

forgiveness

Forgive as the Lord forgave you.

COLOSSIANS 3:13

LORD, THE PRAYER YOU GAVE YOUR DISCIPLES SAYS, "FORGIVE US our debts as we forgive our debtors." Even when I say something stupid and the other kids laugh at me, help me to forgive others the same way You forgive me. Help me to remember what You did when people laughed at You. You didn't get mad, You just forgave them.

Snow

Though your sins

are like scarlet,

they shall be as white as snow.

ISAIAH 1:18

JESUS, WHEN YOU WERE A LITTLE BOY, did it ever snow in Your town? I think snow is one of the neatest things You made. Snow is so white and clean. I can see why You sometimes like to cover up the earth with snow. People do fun things in the snow like sledding and making snowmen and even snow angels. When You forgive me for my sins, it feels like being covered up with snow. It makes me feel clean inside. Thanks for snow.

Hearing God

He who belongs to God
hears what God says.

JOHN 8:47

IT'S SO NEAT TO PRAY TO YOU EVERY NIGHT, JESUS. You're so big, and my voice is so small. I don't understand how You hear me, but I'm sure glad You do. Help me to remember, God, that prayer is not only talking to You but also being quiet so that I can hear You talk back to me. Let me listen carefully to You by reading Your Bible.

The Lord came and stood there, calling as at the
other times, "Samuel! Samuel!" Then Samuel
said, "Speak, for your servant is listening."

1 SAMUEL 3:10

YOU TALKED TO THE PROPHET SAMUEL WHEN HE WAS JUST a little boy. Sometimes I wish my ears could hear Your voice, especially when I have a problem that I don't know how to fix. I like it when You put Your thoughts in my mind. Would You please help me to solve it? It's so neat to pray to You every night, Jesus, thanks!

Filled with God

*You are the light
of the world.*

MATTHEW 5:14

IN MATTHEW 5 JESUS TALKS ABOUT BEING THE LIGHT OF the world. I want to be Your light. Not a little light, like a match that's on fire only for a second, but a warm light that keeps on glowing, like a candle. Help me to glow with Your love when things get dark around me.

*From the fullness of his grace
we have all received
one blessing after another.*

JOHN 1:16

LORD, SOMETIMES I FEEL LIKE I'M EMPTY ON THE INSIDE. I want to be full of love, joy, peace, and all the other fruit of the Spirit, Lord. I want You in my heart, too. I want it to be Your home. I want to believe in You in a bigger way. Tonight, would You fill me up on the inside?

Family

Even to your old age and gray hairs
I am he, I am he who will sustain you.
I have made you and I will carry you.

ISAIAH 46:4

I THINK GRANDMOTHERS AND GRANDFATHERS ARE ONE OF Your best ideas, because they are kind, loving, and fun. But grandmothers and grandfathers need somebody to watch out for them, too. Would You please do that, Lord? Please make a note to care tonight for everyone who has white hair and wrinkles, especially my grandparents. Thank You for being kind and loving to all the grandparents.

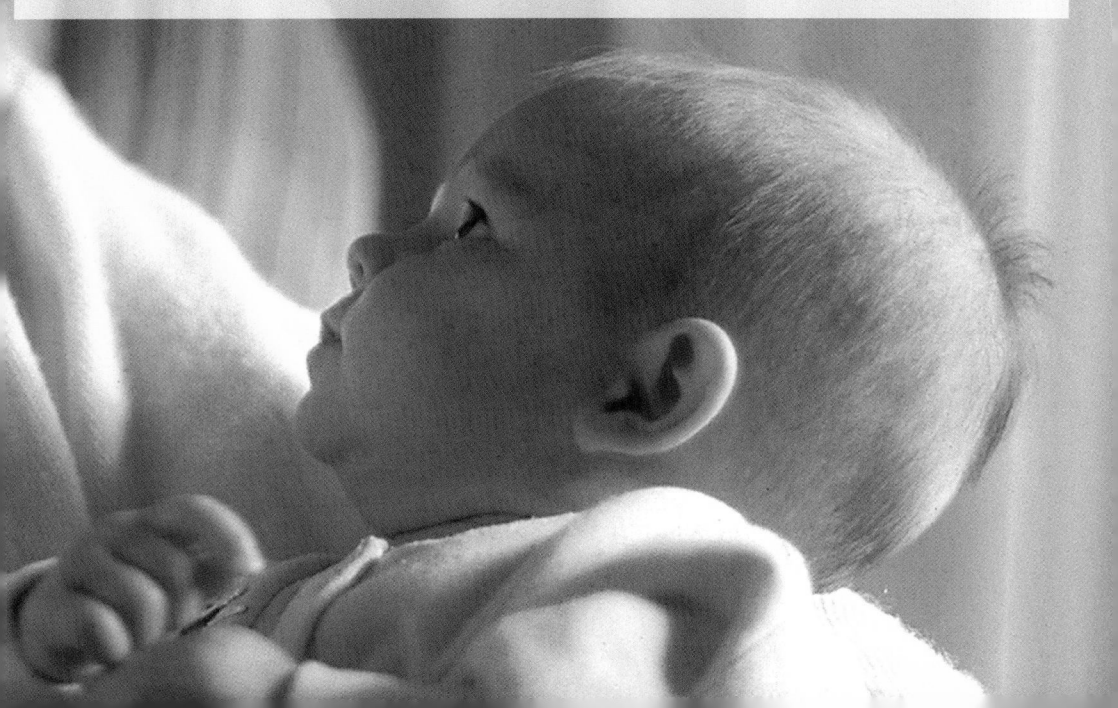

Joy

The joy of the Lord is your strength.

NEHEMIAH 8:10

LORD, IT SEEMS LIKE SUMMER VACATION WILL NEVER COME. I love the way that the summer sky is filled with pretty colors and light. Joy is a gift that You give to people who love You. Please help me to be full of summertime joy even on gloomy winter days.

Helping Others

But the fruit of the Spirit is love, joy, peace, patience, kindness, goodness, faithfulness, gentleness and self-control.

GALATIANS 5:22-23

I LIKE THE STORY YOU TOLD ABOUT THE GOOD SAMARITAN, LORD. He helped someone who was hurting. If I see someone who is hurting tomorrow, would You remind me to be a good Samaritan, too? Help me to do things for other people to make them feel good. Today, Lord, please show me how I can help someone.

God's Help

David said to the Philistine, "You come against me
with sword and spear and javelin, but I come
against you in the name of the Lord Almighty....
All those gathered here will know that it is
not by sword or spear that the Lord saves;
for the battle is the Lord's.

1 SAMUEL 17:45,47

I LIKE THE STORY OF DAVID AND GOLIATH, LORD. THERE ARE problems that seem big in my life, like Goliath. Sometimes I feel small when I look at them like David must have felt. David conquered his big problem with Your help and I can do the same! Help me to be brave like David and trust in God.

Teach us to number our days aright,
that we may gain a heart of wisdom.

PSALM 90:12

PSALM 90 TEACHES ME TO NUMBER MY DAYS. HELP ME TO MAKE each day count for You and look on the bright side of everything. Even when it's rainy, help me to look for rainbows.

No temptation has seized you except what
is common to man. And God is faithful;
he will not let you be tempted
beyond what you can bear.

1 CORINTHIANS 10:13

LORD, KEEP ME FROM WATCHING TV PROGRAMS THAT TEACH things You don't like, talking back to mom or dad, and not doing my chores with a happy heart. Tell my heart when I should change the channel, say kind words, or clean my room. When I get tempted to do or say bad things, help me to remember, God, that with You, saying "no" can be easy.

God Cares for Me

Are not two sparrows sold for a penny?
Yet not one of them will fall
to the ground apart from
the will of your Father.
And even the very hairs of
your head are all numbered.
So don't be afraid;
you are worth more
than many sparrows.

MATTHEW 10:29-31

I LOVE THE STARS! IT'S AMAZING THAT YOU know all their names—zillions of them! Thank You that You know my name, too. You even know how many hairs I have on my head. You must care about me a lot if You know that much about me. It makes me feel important. I want to thank You tonight for caring so much.

Contentment

Be content with what you have, because God has said,
"Never will I leave you; never will I forsake you."

HEBREWS 13:5

LORD, WOULDN'T IT BE NEAT IF I COULD TRADE HOUSES WITH MY friends! I wonder what it would be like to have my best friend's bedroom. Then again, I think I'll stay right where I am. I like my house, Lord. Sometimes I feel like moving away, Lord. Other days I don't ever want to move. Help me to be happy wherever I am.

I have learned to be content whatever the circumstances....
I have learned the secret of being content
in any and every situation.

PHILIPPIANS 4:11-12

LORD, ONCE IN A WHILE I GET JEALOUS OF THINGS OTHER kids have. Dear Lord, I remember being at a birthday party once and feeling jealous because my friend got a neat gift. It was something I really wanted. I'm sorry. You said in the Bible that it's more blessed to give than to receive. Help me to be happy for my friends instead of thinking about myself.

It is more blessed to give than to receive.

ACTS 20:35

LORD, WHENEVER I GET GIFTS, ESPECIALLY AT CHRISTMAS TIME,
help me to not think so much about getting gifts, but giving them.
Help me to be thankful for what You have given me.

Prayer for Poor People

Rescue the weak and needy;
  deliver them from the hand of the wicked.

PSALM 82 TALKS ABOUT RESCUING THE WEAK AND THE NEEDY. You know that there are lots of homeless people in the cities, don't You, Lord? Please help them to find shelter because it's awfully cold on the streets at night. And help the workers in rescue missions to provide beds and blankets.

Peace

I urge, then...that requests, prayers, intercession
  and thanksgiving be made for everyone—
    for kings and all those in authority,
    that we may live peaceful and quiet lives
      in all godliness and holiness.

1 TIMOTHY 2:1-2

TONIGHT I WANT TO PRAY FOR THE LEADER OF OUR COUNTRY and all the important people who help him make decisions. Please guide him, Jesus. Help the people in our country live in peace, and help them to know You.

Bible

Your word is a lamp to my feet

       and a light for my path.

PSALM 119:105

SOMETIMES I HAVE SO MANY QUESTIONS ABOUT ZILLIONS of things. God, I'm glad that the really important answers are in Your big answer book, the Bible! Your words are a "lamp to my feet," Lord. Would You shine Your light brightly on my path so I can see the way You want me to go?

All Scripture is God-breathed and is useful for

      teaching, rebuking, correcting and training

        in righteousness, so that the man of God may be

          thoroughly equipped for every good work.

2 TIMOTHY 3:16

THANK YOU FOR ALL THE IMPORTANT PEOPLE WHO HELPED You write Your message so that it could come to me in the Bible. My Bible has lots of answers in it. Every time I read my Bible, it's like getting a letter from You. My Bible is so special to me, God. I feel like You wrote it just for me.

Every word of God is flawless.

PROVERBS 30:5

I'M GLAD THE BIBLE IS TRUE. IT CONTAINS NO LIES.
God, help me to always tell the truth and to never, ever lie.
I know it's very important to obey You, God. Lord, I want
to memorize a Bible verse tomorrow. Help me to find a verse
I can memorize. (Only please, Lord, make it short!)

Jesus Died for Me

He himself bore our sins in his body on the tree,
so that we might die to sins and live for righteousness;
by his wounds you have been healed.

1 Peter 2:24

TONIGHT, JESUS, I WANT TO THANK YOU FOR DYING ON THE CROSS for me. Thank You for thinking of me when You were on the Cross. I'm glad that because You died on the cross, I can go to heaven. Lord, turn the sad things of my life into something joyful. You did it with Jesus and His cross, thank You for doing it in me.

Following God

Be imitators of God, therefore, as dearly
loved children and live a life of love.

Ephesians 5:1

GOD, TONIGHT I PRAY THAT YOU WOULD MAKE ME MORE like Jesus. When I hear You say "Follow Me," I want to look at following You like an adventure! I'm ready to have You do something new in my life this year. I want to be a good helper to my parents and friendly to everyone around me. Thanks for leading me, I'm ready to follow!

Missionaries

Go and make disciples of all nations...
and teaching them to obey
everything I have commanded you.
And surely I am with you always,
to the very end of the age.

Matthew 28:19-20

Lord, You had a great idea when You made jungles. I love the tigers and the monkeys. But lots of people live in jungles, too. They believe in little gods made of stone and wood. Please help the missionaries there as they talk about You to the people. Help missionaries to reach the tribes in the jungles.

Praying for Others

The prayer of a righteous man

is powerful and effective.

JAMES 5:16

PEOPLE ALL OVER THE WORLD ARE PRAYING, God, and I like to think that my little prayer is being added to theirs. I pray for my neighborhood tonight and all the families in their homes. I pray for all of the kids whose parents don't have jobs. I pray for all the farmers in the country. Please reach out to lonely people and let them know that You love them. Help them to find peace in You. I pray that they will run to You because You are their hiding place.

Church

God placed all things
under [Jesus'] feet and
appointed him to be head
over everything for the church
which is his body.

EPHESIANS 1:22-23

LORD, THE BIBLE SAYS YOU TAUGHT THE teachers in the Temple when You were only twelve. You must have really enjoyed being in church to worship Your Father. I like being in church, too! Thank You for my church. I pray for Sunday school teachers in my church, Lord. They work hard every week and take time just for us. I pray for my pastor, too, because he works really hard, Lord. Please bless him. Thank You for my church; it's really Your church, isn't it?

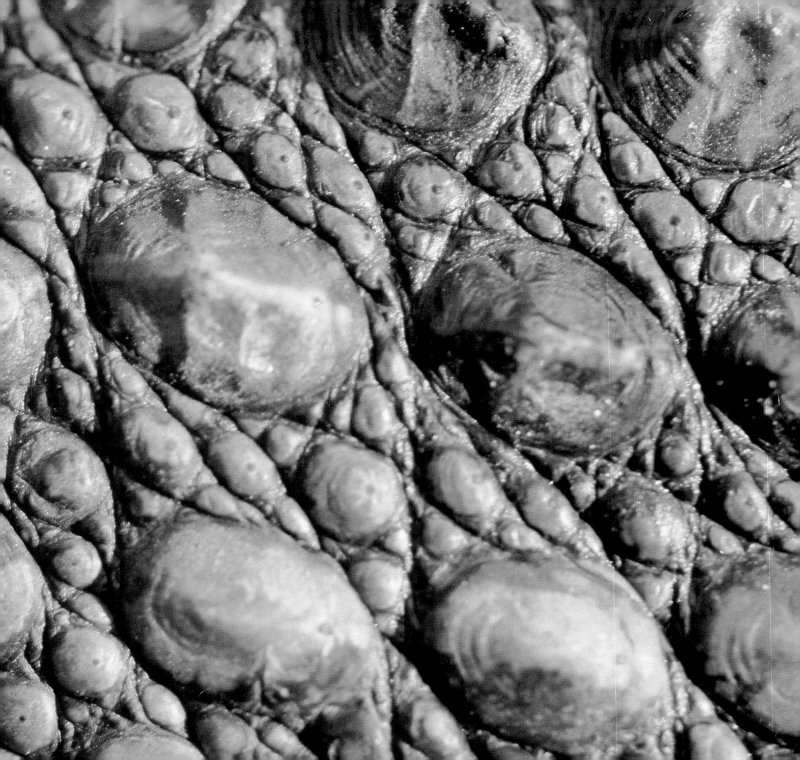

A Michael Neugebauer Book

First published in the United States, Canada, Great Britain, Australia,
and New Zealand in 1994 by North-South Books, an imprint of Nord-Süd Verlag AG.
First paperback edition published in 2000 by North-South Books.

Text and photographs copyright © 1993 by Mark Deeble and Victoria Stone
First published in Switzerland under the title Das Krokodil-Kinder-Buch
by Michael Neugebauer Verlag AG, Gossau Zürich.
The Animal Family series is supervised by biologist Sybille Kalas.

Distributed in the United States by North-South Books Inc., New York.

Deeble, Mark
[Krokodil-Kinder-Buch. English]
The crocodile family book / Mark Deeble, Victoria Stone.
(The Animal family series)
1. Crocodiles—Tanzania—Serengeti National Park—Juvenile literature.
[1. Crocodiles—Tanzania. 2. Serengeti National Park (Tanzania) 3. National parks
and reserves—Tanzania.] I. Stone, Victoria. II. Title. III.Series.
QL666.C925D4313   1994   597.98—dc 20   94-17262

A CIP catalogue record for this book is available from The British Library.
ISBN 1-55858-263-0 (trade edition) 10 9 8 7 6 5 4 3 2 1
ISBN 1-55858-264-9 (library edition) 10 9 8 7 6 5 4 3 2 1
ISBN 0-7358-1317-5 (paperback) 10 9 8 7 6 5 4 3 2 1
Printed in Italy

Mark Deeble

Victoria Stone

The Crocodile Family Book

NORTH-SOUTH BOOKS / NEW YORK / LONDON

Far away in Africa a small river called the Grumeti draws its water from the plains of Tanzania's Serengeti National Park and drains into Lake Victoria. The Grumeti lies just below the equator, so it's hot here all year long. There is no winter, but there are seasons—a wet season, when it rains a lot, and a dry season. After months without rain the Grumeti sometimes stops flowing and for many miles it may dry up completely, leaving only a sandy, tree-lined gully. When it rains in Africa, it rains really hard. As the wet season begins, thunderstorm follows thunderstorm, and flash floods sweep down the Grumeti. Only then, as it pours its muddy waters into Lake Victoria for the next few months, does it really deserve the name "river." It is like a thousand other little rivers on this great continent, and could easily be overlooked if it wasn't for something that makes the Grumeti very special—it is home to the largest crocodiles in Africa.

Grumeti crocodiles are Nile crocodiles, the largest kind in Africa. They can grow to over 20 feet (6 metres) long and weigh well over a ton. In the past, crocodiles were hunted for their skins, which were made into handbags and shoes. Since the largest were the easiest to find and were worth a lot more money, they were the first to be shot. Today, few are longer than 15 feet (about 4.5 metres). Although crocodiles are now protected by law, they grow very slowly, so it will be a long time before many grow to 20 feet (about 6 metres) again.

The Grumeti crocodiles are especially safe because they live in the Serengeti National Park. On a 10-mile (16-kilometre) stretch of the river there are about a thousand crocodiles, from tiny babies to a giant old male who is almost 18 feet (5.5 metres) long. We have made our camp on this part of the river at a place called Kirawira. It takes its name from a poacher who swam across the river to escape the park rangers. He never reached the other side; and to this day the place where the largest crocodiles live is known as Kirawira.

Our story starts early one morning in May on the banks of the Grumeti. It is the end of the wet season and the river is swollen with muddy floodwater. The sandbanks are underwater, so the crocodiles have crowded together on a small island in the middle of the river to bask in the hot sun. Like all reptiles, crocodiles are said to be "cold-blooded," but this doesn't mean that a crocodile's blood is normally cold—it isn't. It's quite warm, like ours. This term just means that crocs can't generate their own body heat, so they need to lie in the sun to warm up. After a night in the river they are quite chilly, so as soon as the sun comes up, they haul themselves out and flop down for a few hours of sunbathing. If they stayed too long in the sun, they would overheat, so towards midday they either slip back into the water or crawl up into the shade. Most of their day is spent like this—either in and out of the water or in and out of the shade. It's a very relaxed lifestyle, and if you walk along the riverbank, it's tempting to think that all the crocodiles lying on the sandbanks are sleeping—but they aren't.

Like the Serengeti's lions, crocodiles are carnivores, which means they eat meat. Like lions, they too are hunters, but instead of chasing their prey, they ambush it. If an animal came down to drink, the apparently sleeping crocodile would slip quietly and slowly into the water and disappear. What happens next? Well, that comes later in the story.

Unlike humans, crocodiles cannot chew or break up food with their hands—so there is no point in a small crocodile trying to catch a large animal. It must catch what it can swallow whole. Baby crocodiles start off eating insects. In the heat of the day, if you are very quiet and still, you can see young crocs trying to sneak up on red dragonflies as they rest on reeds above the water. When the baby crocs grow a little bigger, they hunt freshwater crabs and frogs. After that it's fish, and only after they are full-grown adults will they be ready to eat the larger mammals.

It is later in the day now and most of the crocodiles that were sunbathing are warm enough to go fishing. At this time of year, fish are swimming upstream to spawn. The river is very muddy, so the crocs can't see the fish underwater—but they can feel them. They lie in the fast current with their jaws wide open, set like a trap. If a fish barely touches one of those teeth, the trap is sprung and the jaws crash together. It's a rather hit-or-miss style of hunting, but there's no chasing, and it doesn't require much energy—it's an ambush and that's what crocodiles do best. But what about the biggest crocs? They have been sitting on the riverbank all day. They don't seem interested in fishing, and no animals have come down to drink at the river. Well, we don't have to worry about them if they don't eat today, or this week, or even this month, because they are reptiles. Unlike people, large reptiles can live comfortably without feeding for several months after swallowing one big meal. Just imagine eating a large meal in December and then nothing else until April! How do the crocodiles do this? As we've seen, they conserve energy by resting most of the time, and the energy they need to keep warm comes from the sun instead of their food. This means that one large meal can keep a crocodile going for a long, long time.

The dry season begins in June, and now there is no more rain. Little by little the river starts to dry up. At first it's almost unnoticeable, but if you put a stick in the sand at water level at bedtime, in the morning you will see that the river has dropped almost an inch overnight.

As the plains alongside the river start to dry, the animals come to drink. But the big crocodiles still don't feed, because these animals have lived alongside the crocs all their lives and they are wary. They drink only where it is very shallow, so there is no chance of being ambushed.

One chilly morning something is different. We are used to the sounds and smells of the river—the raucous call of the fish-eagle or the bark of baboons if they are disturbed while picking tamarinds in the tree above our tent. This morning, though, it is still and strangely quiet.

The air is dusty and there is the faint smell of a farmyard. Then we hear a distant rumble. It sounds like a faraway jet or traffic on a busy road on the other side of a hill—but that's impossible in the Serengeti. It's the voices of a hundred thousand wildebeest.

Every year the great herds of wildebeest from the plains in the south of the Serengeti migrate northward in search of fresh grazing; and every year their journey brings them to the banks of the Grumeti River.

This is what the biggest crocs have been waiting for, and as the herds come to drink, the big crocs slip silently into the water and disappear. The wildebeest are hot and thirsty. There is no water left on the plains. Although they have been following the course of the river, before this point its banks have been lined with thick bush and thorn trees, so they have been unable to drink.

The calves are especially thirsty. They are tired from the long journey, and their mothers' milk is beginning to dry up. Even so, they do not rush down to the water, but stand beside their mothers at the top of the bank, bleating in anticipation.

With its head down to drink, legs splayed and feet firmly planted in the mud, a young wildebeest is easy game. A leopard or lion might be lurking in the bushes, so the wildebeest mill and jostle about nervously, each unwilling to be the first to go down to the water. Eventually an old bull, one-horned and limping, walks down to drink. Others follow, and soon the wildebeest line the bank shoulder to shoulder. The strangely shaped "logs" that come floating down with the current mean nothing to them. Even when those logs submerge, the wildebeest do not identify the threat.

Ever so slowly a pair of yellow eyes rises above the muddy water and then disappears. It happens so gradually that there is barely a ripple. The wildebeest notice nothing. Still the crocodiles do not attack. The water close to the bank is too shallow for a successful ambush.

The crocs have waited all year for this opportunity, so why attack too soon and risk frightening away the herd? So they wait…and wait. Then a wildebeest steps farther out into the water. Maybe it was squashed between two others, or perhaps it did not like the muddy water closer to shore. Whatever the reason, that single step into deeper water is all the crocodile needs. He explodes from the water, his great jaws a blur as the wildebeest vanishes in the spray. It's all over in a matter of seconds.

A minute later the crocodile surfaces in midstream, the wildebeest already dead in its mouth. Other crocodiles have sensed the commotion and they hurry towards the disturbance. Ordinarily they would be too frightened to approach the large male that made the capture, but when there is food around, fear is forgotten. The large croc tolerates the others out of need, not generosity. Since crocodiles cannot chew, he cannot break up the body by himself. With lots of crocs hanging on, others can grab hold and then spin around and around to break pieces off.

Now and then a head emerges from the uproar. There is a toothy grin and a flash of white teeth as a chunk of meat is tossed back down the crocodile's throat.

Back on the bank the wildebeest have hardly noticed what has happened. They mill around but don't flee as they would from lions or hyenas. Those closest to the bank haven't even stopped drinking. Their confidence is contagious, and soon the herd is back drinking again.

For a week or so the crocodiles catch a wildebeest every day, and they grow fat and lazy. Very soon they don't even bother to hunt anymore, but lie in the sun sleeping off the huge meal. It's a real feast, but it's probably the only one the large crocodiles will have all year, because as suddenly as the wildebeest herd arrived, it disappears. They will have to make do with a few spiny catfish for twelve months, until the next dry season, when the wildebeest return.

At night now we lie awake and listen to the roars of the giant males as they challenge each other for ownership of the permanent pools. One night there is a terrible fight as two males chase each other along the riverbed beside our camp. In the moonlight we see them wrestle and bite each other in the struggle for dominance. Towards morning the newcomer is driven from the pool and the victorious old male slaps his great jaws together in a prehistoric sound that echoes along the river. This fight was unusual, for normally such contests are settled long before they erupt into violence. As long as the others acknowledge the supremacy of the old male, he will not attack, and the crocodile pool is a surprisingly peaceful and sociable place.

The prospect of a permanent pool with its resident female crocodiles means that the younger male will be back, though perhaps not this year. The old male in the pool near our camp is almost 100 years old and has been king of this stretch of river for perhaps 20 years.

He is almost 18 feet (5.5 metres) long and his massive head is heavily ridged and knobbed. When he hauls himself out of the water and lumbers out onto the sandbank, he stands nearly 3 feet (about 1 metre) high. He has fought off many challengers over the years, and while he shows no scars of combat, others are less lucky. The crocodile in the next pool downstream has lost the end of his top jaw—most likely from a battle with another crocodile.

When we walk down to the pool from our camp, the old male is always the first crocodile we see as he basks or patrols his pool. The females are harder to see, for at this time of year they lie hidden, up in the bushes guarding their nests. Almost 3 months ago the females laid their eggs. Each dug a hole a couple of feet deep and then laid anywhere from 30 to 90 eggs roughly the size of goose eggs, with hard white shells. Once the sand had been replaced, there was nothing to show where the eggs were.

For the next three months the females stay close by, to guard their eggs against hyenas, baboons, and monitor lizards. The monitor lizards are the biggest threat, for they constantly dig test holes up and down the beach, prospecting for eggs.

If a female leaves for even a few minutes, the 3-foot (1 metre) lizards will scuttle in and start digging. Occasionally one is lucky and emerges with an egg in its mouth. Usually, once the nest has been opened it is doomed, because mongooses and baboons will not be far behind.

We have to be careful not to disturb the nesting females, so we stay hidden from view inside a canvas hide, waiting for the eggs to hatch.

At dawn one morning, as we are getting into the hide for the day, we hear a strange noise. It is a muted squeaking, which we hear only when we move. It's very strange—if we stop, it stops. Walking gently over to the nest, we press our ears to the ground and tap the sand. Immediately we are answered by a chorus of tiny squeaks. It's the baby crocodiles calling to their mother! After 3 months in the hot sun, the sand above the nest has baked hard. It's too hard for the baby crocodiles to wriggle through on their own, so now that they are ready to hatch, they are calling their mother to come and release them.

As soon as we are settled in the hide, the mother crocodile emerges from the water. Lying on top of the nest, she starts to dig down with her front feet. It's tiring work and she rests often. With every clawful of sand she clears, the squeaking gets louder. At last, driven on by the cries of her babies, she uncovers the first egg. It hatches instantly, and a perfect miniature crocodile crawls out. It's about 10 inches (25 centimetres) long, and it calls, "Eeoww. Eeoww, eeoww." Try it—it's a short, high-pitched sound. Run the "ee" and the "oww" together, and as you do it, wrinkle up your nose and draw your top lip back—that's the sound that the baby crocodiles make.

As other eggs are uncovered, they also hatch, and soon a small group of babies has collected around the female. Then something extraordinary happens. She looks down and starts to take them into her mouth. At first it appears she is going to eat them, but she doesn't. Very carefully she puts the babies in her mouth. She throws some of them into the air and catches them with the same movement used to eat pieces of meat. (Look carefully at the photo on the opposite page—just in front of the lower jaw of the mother with her mouth open, one of her babies is in midair.) She doesn't swallow them, but the floor of her mouth drops to form a pouch. Before long there are a dozen tiny crocodiles peering out from behind those enormous teeth. They look like prisoners behind bars, but they are inside for their own protection. Once their mother has a mouthful, she carries them down over the beach to the safety of the water. There she releases them close to the reeds.

Back at the nest the predators have homed in, and many of the babies are taken by monitors, eagles, and mongooses before the mother returns. Of the 30 eggs she laid, only 20 tiny crocodiles make it as far as the river. Even there they are not completely safe.

If they stray into deep water, they are in danger of being eaten by large fish such as catfish or the giant Nile perch shown here. They hide in the reeds, but even so there is constant danger from hungry storks, eagles, and snakes.

For the next few weeks the mother will stay close to her babies to guard them. She is a very caring parent, and when she lifts her head above the water, all the babies scramble to get on top, because it's the safest place in the river.

Even when one steps on her eye as it climbs up, she only blinks in a good-natured way. She is very tolerant of this pile of wriggling babies, but eventually even the patience of a crocodile is strained, and she slips below the surface to gain a moment's peace. This upsets her babies, who aren't so used to the water. They are left splashing and rolling around in confusion. As soon as she appears, though, it all starts again, and for the next few weeks she won't get any peace.

But no matter how watchful their mother is, she can't guard all her babies all the time. Some get lost or eaten, others are washed away by the river, and a few weeks after her babies have hatched, only 5 or 6 remain.

It's time for them to set off on their own now, to hunt for themselves and slowly learn the skills they will need if they are going to survive to become adults.

The little ones need to discover what they might eat—and what might eat them—and learn that hippos and even big crocodiles are no friends of small crocodiles. They must find out where to go if the river dries up. Already they have made a good start.

As we watch them jumping up at the red dragonflies that rest on the reeds, we can see them already developing the skills they will need for the rest of their lives. And although they don't know it, the way they are learning to catch dragonflies today—the slow stalk and sudden strike—is the same ambush they will use in 30 years' time, when they are big enough to catch wildebeest.

As dusk falls and we prepare to go back to our camp, we take one last look around, using flashlights. If we hold our lights alongside our heads, we can see the reflections of the eyes of the baby crocodiles, like so many glowing coals, from their hiding places close to the bank.

They have a long way to go, but perhaps one will make it. Perhaps if your grandchildren come to these pools on the Grumeti in 80 years' time and see a giant male crocodile who rules the river—who knows? He might be one of those tiny babies we saw carried down to the water, so gently, all those years ago.

The Animal Family Series

The Animal Family books are not just written by their authors. They are studied and researched and lived into existence. When the authors travel around the world to study, children go right along with them, profiting from the naturalists' firsthand knowledge and experiences in the field. Each book in the Animal Family series helps to make the world of nature that much more real, more understandable, and more valuable to children everywhere.

Ask your bookseller for these other Animal Family books:

THE BEAVER FAMILY BOOK
THE CHIMPANZEE FAMILY BOOK
THE DESERT FOX FAMILY BOOK
THE ELEPHANT FAMILY BOOK
THE GOOSE FAMILY BOOK
THE GRIZZLY BEAR FAMILY BOOK
THE LEOPARD FAMILY BOOK
THE LION FAMILY BOOK
THE PENGUIN FAMILY BOOK
THE POLAR BEAR FAMILY BOOK
THE WHALE FAMILY BOOK
THE WILD HORSE FAMILY BOOK

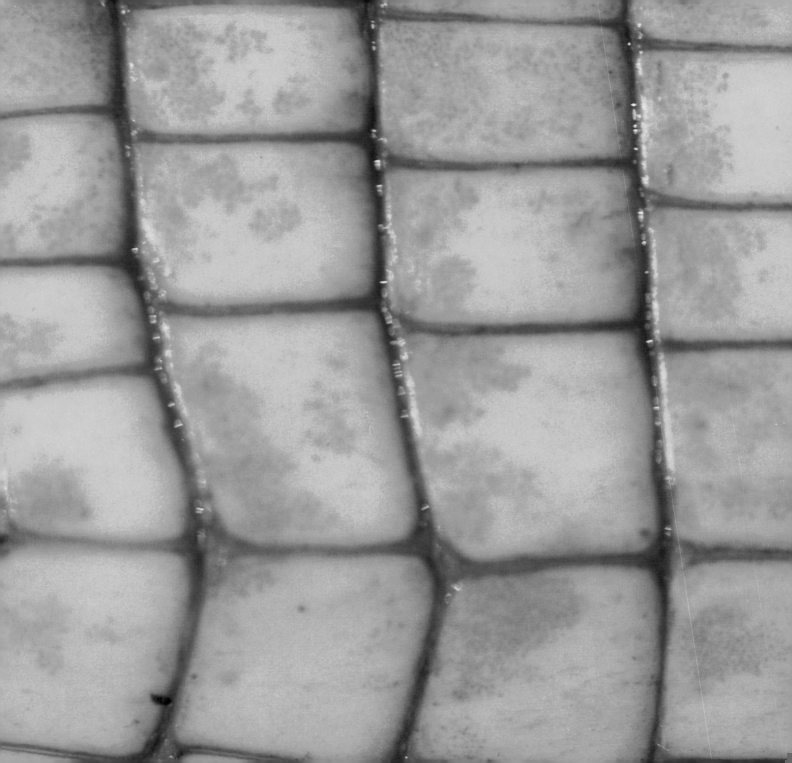